Zoo

Written by **Alison Hawes**

Contents

Early zoos	4
Zoos today	6
A better life?	10
Free to roam?	14
Helping animals in danger	18
What do you think about zoos?	22
Contacts	24

Early zoos

There have been zoos for thousands of years.

The first zoo kept camels, lions, bears and lynx.

Did you know?

The first zoo in the UK was started by King William II, over 900 years ago!

In 1250, King Henry III moved the Royal Zoo to London.

An elephant was given to the zoo in 1254, by the King of France.
Many people who saw it, thought it was a trick!
They couldn't believe it was a real animal!

The zoo had a polar bear,
which was allowed to swim in the Thames
on the end of a long rope!

Zoos today

Today there are thousands of zoos where people can see animals from many different countries.
If there were no zoos very few people would ever see the wonderful animals that live in different parts of the world.

Did you know?

The biggest zoo in the world is in San Diego in the USA. It is home to over 4,000 animals!

The smallest animals in the zoo are leaf cutter ants.
They can carry a leaf five times heavier than themselves!

The largest animal in the zoo is an African elephant called Tembo.
He weighs as much as four cars!

Sometimes you can get *really close* to zoo animals.
But you may not want to get *this* close to a snake!

Many people think that zoos are good places to learn about wild animals.
Zoo keepers often give talks about the animals they look after.

This child is being a zoo keeper for the day!

BUT ...

Some zoos keep animals in very small cages.
Sometimes the animals can hardly move.
Some zoos keep animals chained up,
with nothing to do.
This can drive the animals insane!

At a zoo in Bali, a monkey was found in a cage so small he could not lie down!

A Japanese bear park

Did you know?

Some people are trying to have zoos like this shut down.

In Japanese bear parks, bears are kept together in empty pits.
People who come to see the bears are allowed to throw food for them.
This causes fights and many of the bears get badly hurt.

A better life?

Some people think animals have a better life in a zoo. In fact, animals often live longer in zoos than they do in the wild.

Lions may die if they are injured in a fight, in the wild.

Did you know?

Lions usually live for 15 years in the wild but up to 30 years in zoos!

Animals can go hungry in the wild.
But zoo animals are well fed.

In zoos, Komodo dragons are fed on dead mice and rats and minced turkey.

Animals in the wild can die if they get sick or injured.
But zoo animals are cared for by vets.

Did you know?

Most lion cubs in the wild die of starvation.

Many zoos try to make life as natural as possible for the animals.

This bear's food has been hidden. It has to search for it, like it does in the wild.

Animals that swim, like tigers, are given pools.
Animals that dig, like meerkats, are given sandy soil to burrow in.
Animals that climb, like monkeys, are given trees, bars and ropes.

The polar bears in San Diego zoo sometimes have real snow blown into their enclosure!

It is against the law to kill many wild animals but many thousands of animals are still killed in the wild, every year.
But zoo animals are safe from hunters.

Tiger skins and bones can be sold for lots of money. Tiger bones are sold to make tiger bone wine!

Rhinos are killed for their horns. One horn can be sold for £50,000!

Free to roam?

Animals in zoos are not free.
Some people think animals have the right to be free.

In the wild, gorillas spend most of their day eating and looking for food.

Did you know?

Gorillas never stay in the same place for more than one day!

Zoos cannot give animals all the space they have in the wild.
They are not free to roam as far as they want.

Did you know?

In the wild, bears roam over hundreds of kilometres.
But in zoos they may only have hundreds of metres to move about in!

A forest as big as Wales would only be big enough for 40 bears!

In the wild, animals are free to hunt their own food.

Polar bears travel for miles looking for food.
They can smell a seal on the ice 20 miles away!

Zoo animals do not go hungry but they are not free to hunt for their own food, every day.

In the wild, pandas live on their own most of the time but in zoos they have to live with other pandas.

In the wild, some animals naturally like to live on their own.
Some are happier living in groups.
But zoo animals are not always free to do this.

In the wild, wildebeest can live in groups of over 1,000!

Helping animals in danger

The last dodo died in 1680.

There are no dodos left now. Most of them were killed by hunters. Animals that die out, like the dodos, are said to be *extinct*.

Wild boar became extinct in Britain about 400 years ago.

Did you know?

Today over 5,000 different kinds of animal are at risk of becoming extinct! This is because people are killing them or destroying the places where they live.

About 100 years ago, there were just 100 bison in the world.
But now, thanks to zoos, there are thousands of bison back in the wild.

Zoos are helping to save animals from extinction. They help by breeding animals and then putting them back in the wild.

Bison, white rhinos and Arabian oryx have all been saved by zoos.

Arabian oryx live in the deserts in Oman.
They can go for nearly two years without a drink!

BUT ...

Only a *few* animals can be put back into the wild by zoos.
Many more animals can be helped by protecting them in reserves in the wild.

Did you know?

It is not just big animals, like pandas and whales, that need protecting.
Small animals, like the bumble bee bat and the no-eyed big-eyed wolf spider need protection too!

No-eyed big-eyed wolf spiders are blind.
They live in complete darkness in caves in Hawaii.
People aren't allowed to disturb the spiders.

To protect animals in the wild, we have to protect the places where they live.

About an acre of rainforest is destroyed every second!
As the forest disappears, millions of animals and plants die.

In 2002, an oil tanker spilled oil into the sea near Spain. More than 200,000 birds were killed.

What do you think about zoos?

If animals could talk, what do you think they would say about zoos?

Should animals be kept in zoos?
Or should they live in the wild?

Are zoos good for animals?
Or should they be closed down?

What do *you* think?

If zoos are closed, will more people visit animals in the wild?

And if more people visit animals in the wild, won't this just destroy the places where animals are safe?

What do *you* think?

Contacts

General animal conservation:
World Wide Fund for Nature
Panda House
Godalming
Surrey
GU7 IBR

http://www.wwf.org.uk

Preservation of habitats:
Born Free Foundation
3 Grove House
Foundry Lane
Horsham
West Sussex
RHI3 5PL

http://www.bornfree.org.uk

Animal welfare in zoos:
World Society for the Protection of Animals (WSPA)
89 Albert Embankment
London SEI 7TP

http://www.wspa.org.uk

Endangered species:
International Union for Conservation of Nature's Red list of endangered and threatened animals and plants:

http://www.redlist.org

Online Good Zoo Guide at:
http://www.goodzoos.com

San Diego Zoo:
http://www.sandiegozoo.org

Jersey Wildlife Preservation Trust:
http://www.durrell.org